A STEP-BY-STEP BOOK ABOUT
STICK INSECTS

DAVID ALDERTON

All photography by the author, unless otherwise indicated.

Humorous drawings by Andrew Prendimano.

Title page: Fully grown female stick insect. Photo by Michael Gilroy.

Distributed in the UNITED STATES by T.F.H. Publications, Inc., One T.F.H. Plaza, Neptune City, NJ 07753; in CANADA to the Pet Trade by H & L Pet Supplies Inc., 27 Kingston Crescent, Kitchener, Ontario N2B 2T6; Rolf C. Hagen Ltd., 3225 Sartelon Street, Montreal 382 Quebec; in CANADA to the Book Trade by Macmillan of Canada (A Division of Canada Publishing Corporation), 164 Commander Boulevard, Agincourt, Ontario M1S 3C7; in ENGLAND by T.F.H. Publications, PO Box 15, Waterlooville PO7 6BQ; in AUSTRALIA AND THE SOUTH PACIFIC by T.F.H. (Australia) Pty. Ltd., Box 149, Brookvale 2100 N.S.W., Australia; in NEW ZEALAND by Ross Haines & Son, Ltd., 82 D Elizabeth Knox Place, Panmure, Auckland, New Zealand; in the PHILIPPINES by Bio-Research, 5 Lippay Street, San Lorenzo Village, Makati, Rizal; in SOUTH AFRICA by Multipet Pty. Ltd., P.O. Box 35347, Northway, 4065, South Africa. Published by T.F.H. Publications, Inc. Manufactured in the United States of America by T.F.H. Publications, Inc.

Contents

INTRODUCTION

Stick insects make fascinating pets for people of all ages. They are easily accommodated and will breed quite readily in the home. For the keen naturalist, there is also plenty of scope to the study of these interesting invertebrates, as much still remains to be learned about their habits. Indeed, out of the 2500 or so species, fewer than 100 have been kept, and probably less than 20 are readily available at present.

Once you have gained experience with the more common species, you may want to become involved in breeding projects with the rarer stick insects. There is a special organization, called the Phasmid Study Group, which is involved in co-ordinating projects of this type.

WHAT ARE STICK INSECTS?

Stick insects belong to a group known to zoologists as the Phasmatodea. This name originates from the Latin word *phasma*, which means 'ghost', and refers to the highly developed camouflage skills of these insects. Stick insects tend to be various shades of green and brown, which help them to blend with the plants on which they are normally found. In addition, some species are also able to change colour to suit their background. The twig-like shape of most stick insects enhances their disguise. In the species known as the Javanese, this camouflage is developed so that the stick insect's body appears to be covered in greenish growths, which in this instance resemble moss or lichen.

Interestingly, the other group of insects classified with the stick insects in the order Phasmatodea has evolved a similar line of defence. But the leaf insects (*Phyllium* species) have a very flattened body shape, which in appearance is more similar to leaves than twigs or sticks. Although less commonly available than stick insects, they need similar care.

Facing Page: Stick insects make fascinating pets for people of all ages.

Stick insects are very agile. They have both claws and sucker pads on their feet, so they are quite capable of climbing a vertical surface such as the side of a glass tank, and they can walk upside down without difficulty. As a result of such behavior, stick insects have become better known in North America as walking sticks. Some species tend to be more active at night, when their movements become less evident to potential predators.

Apart from their shape and coloration, stick insects have a variety of other means that help to conceal their presence. In the open, they can rock back and forth on their legs, resembling twigs blown about in a slight breeze. Alternatively, they can adopt a rigid stance, remaining immobile for many minutes. Some stick insects, such as the Indian, can also fold their legs and fall down, feigning death when they are touched. Known technically as catalepsy, this behaviour often deters potential predators.

Stick insects may respond in several other ways to direct contact, depending upon the species concerned. Some, such as the Pink-winged, have wings that enable them to fly off when threatened. Although not especially powerful on the wing, they can effectively escape by this means. You must therefore be careful with these stick insects if you take them outside to clean their quarters, since they can disappear with relative ease, especially in a gust of wind.

As a further refinement, stick insects such as the Javanese have bright wing colours that are normally hidden when the wing is closed. The sudden flash of colour when the insect takes off suggests that it could be poisonous. Most brightly coloured insects are ignored by potential predators for this reason.

A similar line of defence is also utilised by immature stick insects, which are known as nymphs. After hatching from its egg, each nymph undergoes a series of moults. During the early part of their life, some nymphs actually curl the rear of the abdomen over the top of their body, appearing similar to a venomous scorpion; as a result, they are likely left unmolested by potential predators. Such behaviour is most noticeable in the case of the Giant Prickly Stick Insect, which has a relatively broad body shape.

Close examination of the larger species in particular reveals the number of spikes protecting the whole body. You can see these better with a magnifying glass. They obviously provide a further deterrent to direct handling. Such spikes are best developed in the case of males of the *Eurycantha* species. On the upper femoral part of each of the back legs there is a long sharp spike. Should you place a finger between its legs, the stick insect will likely close its legs instinctively, driving these spines into your finger with painful consequences. On New Guinea and the neigh-

The stick insect's camouflage is one of its keys to survival. This female Jungle Nymph demonstrates just how effective its camouflage can be.

bouring islands where these stick insects are found, fishermen actually collect them for their sharp spines, which are used as fishhooks.

A few stick insects also have chemical defences, but not all are well known in collections. The Florida Stick (*Anisomorpha buprestoides*) needs to be handled with particular care, as it produces an unpleasant spray from glands in the vicinity of the head. If this spray enters your eyes, a painful reaction will occur. The resulting swelling takes a couple of days to subside, although the effects, including blindness, are only temporary.

Obviously, avoid handling this species close to your face. Should you be unlucky enough to be sprayed, immediately flush your eye with plenty of cold water to dilute its effects, then seek medical advice. Clearly, this species is not recommended for children or novice keepers.

Some stick insects produce chemical secretions that actually give off a pleasant odour. The scent of the Javanese is reputedly like that of perfume, but inhalation of it can cause you to sneeze.

STICK INSECT PLAGUES

In spite of so many defences, phasmid populations rarely build up to plague proportions in the wild. They face a whole host of predators, ranging from other invertebrates to birds and mammals. As one example, the introduction of rats to Lord Howe Island, off the eastern coast of Australia, resulted in the near extinction of the phasmid population there. Among the most unusual predators of stick insects are the various cleptid wasps (*Myrmecomimesis* species), the females of which actually seek out phasmid eggs and lay their own eggs in them. The young wasps then feed on the phasmid eggs, preventing their development.

Tachinid flies, in contrast, attack both nymphs and adult stick insects. The larvae develop within the phasmids' bodies in this instance. Thankfully, however, such problems are not likely to be encountered by the stick insect keeper, because of the very specialised way in which these invertebrates attack their hosts.

On occasions in the wild, however, stick insects have become notable pests in their own right. One of the worst outbreaks on record occurred during 1963, in southern Australia, when an area of 650 sq.miles (168,349 ha) of eucalyptus forest was stripped of leaves by stick insects, with a number of the trees failing to recover.

A sequence of factors underlies population explosions of this type. First, it is often the case that the woodland has not been exposed to forest fires for a decade or more. The absence of fires allows the phasmid population to build up over successive generations and ensures good vegetative cover in the area as well. Additionally, the temperature of the region must also be conducive to the hatching of eggs.

Studies suggest that following an explosion in the phasmid population, birds that feed mainly on insects, such as the Pied Currawong (*Strepera graculina*) move into the area. In the following year, there is then likely to be a resulting population crash.

Although the stick insects will have produced more eggs than before, there will be far less vegetation available for the resulting nymphs. The majority of them are then destined to starve to death or fall victim to predators, which increased in numbers during the previous explosion.

Some serious outbreaks have been recorded in parts of the United States and in the Pacific, where coconut plantations were attacked. Wherever you live, you should take care to ensure that none of your stick insects escape into the wild. Otherwise they could possibly establish themselves, and they might even become economic pests.

You can find two species of New Zealand stick insects living wild in parts of southwestern England. It is believed that they were introduced there with plants during the early part of the twentieth century. They are known to occur on the Scilly Isles, and in Devon and Cornwall, where the climate is also relatively mild. *Acanthoxyla prasina* can be distinguished from *Clitarchus hookeri* by the presence of spines on its head and thorax.

Mantids are distantly related to the stick insects. But beware, for many mantids will prey on stick insects. Photo by M. Gilroy of dead leaf mantis, *Deroplatys dessiccata*.

BASIC ANATOMY

The stick insect's body can be divided into three parts. At the front end, there is the head, with two protruding antennae that have a sensory function. The thorax forms the middle section of the body, and in turn is subdivided into three segments. The relatively short prothorax has the first pair of legs attached to it. This is followed by the mesothoracic segment, and then the metathorax–both of which also have pairs of legs attached to them, as well as the wings, if present. The abdomen forms the final part of the stick insect's body. At its rear, the genital opening is

The three basic parts of the stick insect's body can be easily seen on this Giant Spiny.

Stick insects feast on a variety of plants, and, in captivity, derive great pleasure in scaling cut branches. Photo by M. Gilroy.

apparent. The three pairs of legs are also segmented, rather like the body. Their shape varies in accordance with the species concerned. The legs of the Indian Stick Insect are relatively thin, whereas those of the Giant Spiny have broad decorative edges which assist camouflage.

The sharp spikes on the legs of some species have already been mentioned. But you will also need to bear in mind that the legs of most stick insects are very fragile. Rough handling will result in the loss of part or all of the leg.

OBTAINING STICK INSECTS

Although many pet shops do not stock stick insects routinely, they will almost certainly be able to obtain them for you. Alternatively, you could contact entomological dealers who advertise in various natural history publications. Those who offer butterflies and moths usually have stick insects available as well.

Another means of supply is to join the Phasmid Study Group. They have a Livestock Co-ordinator who arranges the distribution of surplus eggs, nymphs and adults to other members of the group. There is also a members' panel, which usually has stock of the more common species available, with the only condition being that you not sell the stock obtained through the group.

It is preferable to start with nymphs that have already moulted several times. Eggs may take months to hatch, and the young nymphs can be difficult to rear in some cases through their first few weeks of life. By the time they are older, however, they will be feeding well. Older nymphs are also easier to handle, and are not as subject to injury. In contrast, adult stick insects may only live for a few months or even weeks after you obtain them. Unless you are left with some eggs, it can indeed prove a brief encounter.

An additional advantage of starting with nymphs is that, if they are missing any limbs, likely these parts will be regenerated at the next moult. Rough handling and overcrowding (leading to cannibalism) can result in loss of limbs. Limbs are not replaced in adults, which are then likely to be handicapped when feeding and moving around their quarters.

When you are looking at a group of stick insects, it is best not to purchase any with missing legs if possible. On rare occasions, you may also see individuals with twisted bodies, and these insects should also be avoided, as they may encounter difficulty when moulting. This applies especially in the case of young nymphs that have hatched from eggs kept in an excessively dry environment and may not have been able to free themselves properly from their egg cases as a result.

Depending on where you live, it is often possible to purchase eggs and also mature stick insects by mail-order. They must be packed

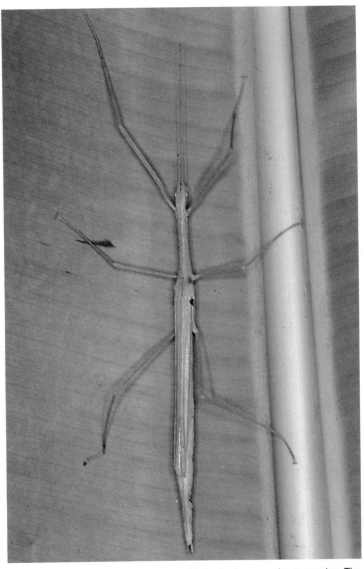

Stick insects vary in their appearance and behavior from species to species. The Pink-winged Stick Insect is a rather dainty creature and one of the stick insects that can fly. Photo by M. Gilroy.

properly in accordance with current postal regulations. In practical terms, this usually means housing them in a secure and stout container, complete with a source of food for the duration of their journey.

The outer packaging should be labelled to reveal the contents of the parcel, and the stick insects should be dispatched by the quickest means of delivery. Eggs, of course, are easier to dispatch, since they take up less space and require no supplemental food.

Should you arrange to collect stick insects yourself, it is a good idea to prepare a suitable travelling box for them. An empty, clean plastic container, complete with a lid, will suffice for this purpose. You can place a quantity of the food plant within. Remember to include some ventilation holes in the lid of the container.

Keep the stick insects in a cool part of the car, under a seat for example, rather than on the back seat in direct sunlight, for the duration of the journey. It is probably best not to place them in the boot (trunk) of the car, just in case there is a leak of exhaust fumes into the chamber, which could harm them. Stick insects are excellent travellers which show no ill-effects from a car journey. Indeed, it has even been suggested that a car trip can encourage mating behaviour in some species, notably the Giant Spiny!

It is important to remember that while some stick insects can be kept at room temperature, others may need additional heating if they are to thrive, so their care is slightly more involved.

In addition, if you are interested in breeding stick insects, you may prefer to concentrate on the parthenogenetic species, which can breed without mating.

Finally, and perhaps most significantly, you should consider the feeding habits of the species in question. It is not a good idea to start with stick insects that are fastidious in terms of the plants on which they feed, unless, for example, you have a good supply of rhododendron leaves available for them.

Facing Page: The Indian Stick Insect has a basically similar cylindrical body shape to the Pink-winged, but it cannot fly.

Before acquiring your stick insects, it is important to prepare their accommodation. A number of options are available, depending partly on the species concerned. You may need to provide very spacious surroundings if you decide to keep some of the larger species, such as the Jungle Nymph. It is important to remember that stick insects need sufficient space if they are to moult without difficulty. In practical terms, this means that they must be able to hang upside down easily, to break out of their old skin. The height of their accommodation must therefore be at least twice as great as their length, as a general guide.

HOUSING

CONVERTED AQUARIA

Adequate ventilation is a very important consideration in the design of housing for stick insects. Proper ventilation will retard the development of moulds, which can otherwise harm the eggs as well as the adult insects. Although an aquarium may appear to offer an obvious and attractive means of housing, the use of the standard aquarium hood for covering the tank does not permit sufficient ventilation. Fortunately, your pet shop carries secure, well-ventilated hoods specially designed for aquariums that house non-aquatic animals. Such hoods are often used for tarantulas and other invertebrates, and are quite suitable for many stick insects as well.

Acrylic tanks are becoming increasingly popular in both the aquatic and terrestrial hobbies today, and these tanks are much lighter than the glass ones. They will also prove more robust, although the plastic surface does tend to scratch quite easily. For large stick insects, such as the Jungle Nymph, a large aquarium provides a good means of housing.

SMALL ANIMAL 'CARRIERS'

Rather new on the pet market are plastic 'small animal carriers,' for lack of a better name. These carriers were originally conceived to temporarily house small animals, such as hamsters and gerbils; reptiles,

Facing Page: Stick insects can make ideal pets for children, provided that proper parental supervision is given at all times.

such as anoles; and invertebrates, such as tarantulas. However, since finding their place on the market, these 'carrying' devices have increased both in form and utility, and many models today can well serve as permanent homes for many of the smaller stick insects. As already noted, size is of paramount importance in determining the accommodation of the stick insect, and owners who consider the small animal carrier as their stick insect's accommodation must strongly consider their animal's space requirements.

Among the advantages of the small animal carrier for housing the smaller stick insects include its low cost, compact size, easy cleanablity, and portable nature. Owners considering this type of accommodation should see their local pet shop for more information.

OTHER HOUSING OPTIONS

It is quite possible for the keeper to construct a whole unit for stick insects using nylon netting on a wooden framework. (Black netting is preferable because it gives better visibility than white once the unit is completed.) However, unless you have considerable handyman skills and an abundance of free time, what you can build can most likely be purchased for less money, not to mention less time and effort. Additionally, home-constructed models are nearly always of wood and other such components, and these products are not nearly as hygienic or easily cleaned as the glass and plastic ones that are purchased. Nonetheless, for the sake of information, a brief discussion of the homemade accommodation is presented.

You can design a suitable accommodation using 1in (0.625cm) wood. While small panel pins can be used to assemble the framework, it is usually simpler just to glue the ends together with a suitable adhesive. Construct each of the four sides separately, with the two opposing sides, of course, being of equal size, and all four of equal height.

With the sides complete, you can then screw or glue them together. Then construct the top in a similar fashion, making sure that it provides a tight fit. It is useful to hinge the top, rather than one of the sides, to act as a door, as there is then less risk of the stick insects escaping while you service their quarters.

The base of the unit is best made of a thin piece of plywood which can be tacked into the bottom of the frame to create a secure structure.

Once the structure has dried thoroughly, cover each surface with nylon netting. Start at one end, being sure that the netting is fixed squarely on top of the frame. Fix it in place using a staple gun. Then pull the netting taut over the rest of the frame, ensuring that it does not sag. Although this will not be harmful to the stick insects in any way, it rather spoils the finished effect once the unit is completed.

A homemade vivarium that can properly accommodate stick insects. Note the vents on both sides of the setup, which allow for good cross-ventilation, and the sliding floor, which allows for easy clean-up.

When it is square and taut on the frame, tack the opposite end of the netting in place, again with staples, and fix the sides in a similar way. Finally, you will probably need to trim the edges of the netting itself with a pair of scissors, removing any excess around the edges of the framework.

The advantage of this type of accommodation is that it provides a relatively cheap means of housing a large collection of stick insects, and it is totally flexible in the size of unit.

EMERGENCY AND BREEDING HOUSING OPTIONS

A wide variety of containers can be used on a temporary basis for holding stick insects. One of the most popular is a clean, empty sweets jar. It can provide adequate depth, but often too little space. Ventilation can also be a problem, and small holes must be punctured in the lid. In contrast, you may be able to find commercially available housing and breeding units specially designed for stick insects.

Depending on your carpentry skills, it is of course possible to design a more elaborate wooden enclosure for breeding stock. In this instance, the sides of the unit apart from the front and roof should be made of thin plywood, with clips being placed on one of them. These clips will ultimately serve to hold the vessel containing the stick insects' food.

By designing the front of the enclosure so that it is slightly shorter, you can then set a sliding tray on the floor to enable you to clean out the quarters easily, without having to disturb the stick insects.

A cage of this type is an ideal breeding accommodation for the larger species which scatter their eggs at random over the floor. You can easily remove these eggs every day for incubation elsewhere. The insects' droppings can be discarded at the same time, reducing the risk of mould affecting the eggs.

Giant Prickly nymph. Despite their camouflage and mimicking skills, nymphs of all stick insect species are susceptible to predation and must be properly accommodated.

Improper heating and/or lighting can affect the stick insect's feeding behavior.

HEATING

Some species of stick insects do need the provision of artificial heat if they are to thrive. A number of breeders use light bulbs for this purpose, but there are several drawbacks to this method of heating. In the first place, the bulb itself must be very carefully screened, because otherwise the stick insects are likely to climb onto the bulb and burn themselves badly.

In addition, even with subdued lighting, using a blue bulb for example, the natural rhythm of darkness and light may be compromised. This could affect the stick insects' feeding behaviour, bearing in mind that many species are nocturnal and tend to be more active in dark surroundings.

In addition, a tungsten light bulb provides a very concentrated source of heat. This in turn dries the atmosphere, leaving the stick insects at greater risk of dehydration. Safety factors must also be considered, because should any moisture fall on a hot bulb when you spray the quarters, it is likely to explode. There is also a potential fire risk if you use combustible materials such as cardboard in the construction of the unit.

21

Should you nevertheless decide to use a tungsten light bulb, then fit it within a metal hood as supplied for fish tanks, or preferably a ventilated vivarium lid intended primarily for keeping reptiles. These will fit over the top of aquaria and are produced in various sizes. A fine mesh grill should prevent the stick insects from getting too close to the heat source. You must also include a thermometer in their quarters, to ensure that the stick insects do not become too hot.

Within such a confined space, only a small low-wattage bulb will be required. Unfortunately, since they are not normally designed to hang upside down, such bulbs often have a very short lifespan in these surroundings. It is of course possible to connect a bulb to a thermostat, but here the constant switching of the light on and off as the temperature falls and rises means that, again, the longevity of the bulb is likely to be compromised.

HEATING PADS

Certainly, the best option now available for heating the stick insects' quarters is in the form of a very thin heating pad that actually fits on a bed of polystyrene beneath the stick insects' accommodation. These bendable, sheet-like heaters are exceedingly durable and reliable. They are available in a wide range of sizes, and, apart from glass, they are also capable of heating effectively through a .6in (1.5cm) chipboard or ply-wood base. In addition, they are inexpensive to operate, although they do need to be connected to a reliable thermostat, which actually controls their heat output. A temperature setting within the range of 70–80°F (21–27°C) will be suitable for most stick insects. Incidentally, this type of heater can also be very useful for speeding up the breeding cycle. It will shorten the time taken for the eggs to hatch and is very safe to operate on a continuous basis.

FLOOR LININGS

Although newspaper is a rather unattractive floor covering, it is quite absorbent and easy to replace. Obviously, sheets of plain white paper are another possible alternative, and especially useful on the floor of cages housing breeding stick insects as the white coloration makes it much easier to spot the eggs.

In the majority of cases, the stick insects will spend most of their time either on the plants within their quarters or climbing around the interior of the cage. But the Giant Spiny and other *Eurycantha* species will often rest on the floor and need cover there. Peat may be used for this purpose, concealing the dark brown bodies of adults quite effectively. You can also include curved pieces of cork bark, which provide additional retreats for the insects, which may spend much of their time hiding there.

Indian Stick Insect exploring a stalk. Photo by M. Gilroy.

Proper housing helps to ensure proper moulting. Moulted skin of a Giant Spiny Stick Insect.

Sphagnum moss can also be included in one corner. If sprayed regularly, the moss will help increase the humidity within the quarters.

HOUSING GUIDELINES

Stick insects vary quite widely in shape and size, and although all are essentially herbivorous in their feeding habits, it is clearly inadvisable to mix delicate species with more robust individuals. In addition, those which are known to produce toxins should be kept on their own, as they could harm others.

Certainly if they are overcrowded, the stick insects are likely to damage each other's legs. Some males are also highly aggressive, espe-

24

cially in the case of *Eurycantha* species, and are best accommodated in breeding pairs or groups with only a few males present. As the young stick insects grow, you may need to separate them into smaller groups, giving them more space.

In the case of species that mate, you should ensure that pairs are established before the adult moult, because mating often takes place soon after moulting occurs for the final time. Pairing them beforehand increases the likelihood of successful breeding.

The legs of some stick insects are enlarged for camouflage purposes, as shown here on this fully grown male stick insect. Photo by M. Gilroy.

Although stick insects feed on a wide variety of plants in the wild, they have proven very adaptable in terms of their diet in captivity. They feed almost exclusively on leaves, and, provided that you have access to a supply of bramble (blackberry) leaves throughout the year, you should have no difficulty in maintaining most species.

FEEDING AND CARE

Bramble grows quite widely, both in semi-wooded and open areas. It can spread by underground root stock, and this means that it is quite easy to establish your own supplies. These will be especially valuable during the colder months of the year, particularly in periods of snowfall, when finding food plants outdoors can be very difficult. A sharp pair of secateurs (pruning shears) and gardening gloves to protect against the sharp thorns will be needed.

ENSURING A REGULAR SUPPLY

You will need a trowel and several large flowerpots. Look for vigorous shoots emerging above ground some distance from the main plant. Start by carefully excavating the root stock of such shoots. Some distance back towards the main plant, sever the underground root, and dig out the shoot with a portion of the root attached. Plant this in the pot; ordinary garden soil can be used for this purpose. Keep the shoot well watered and in a relatively sheltered and shaded position. Soon it should be growing well.

You can then start to train the shoot so that it develops into a more compact bush. Start by pinching off the tip of the shoot. This in turn will encourage side shoots to sprout at the junction of the individual leaves. The plant can be trained up canes so that the leaves remain clean. By careful trimming, not only will you then have a supply of food for your stick insects, but the bramble will grow into a more productive shape.

Facing Page: Close-up view of the mouth parts of a fully grown female stick insect. Photo by M. Gilroy.

Avoid cutting young shoots, however, as some stick insects, especially nymphs, do not thrive on the small leaves. It has been suggested that there could be a toxic compound of some kind present in them, although, in other parts of the world, stick insects have proved highly adept at overcoming the effects of plant toxins. Certain species, such as *Oreophoetes peruanas*, have even evolved to feed on ferns that contain powerful chemical deterrents of this type.

PICKING BRAMBLE

When you are collecting bramble in the wild, try to avoid areas where chemicals may be used. Hedgerows close to roads or in the vicinity of playing fields are potentially dangerous collecting sites. Choose bramble leaves that are green, not brown at the edges and dying back, as the stick insects will find these unpalatable.

If some of the leaves on a stem are showing signs of age, trim them back so that the edges are fresh. This trimming is especially important when feeding young nymphs, which otherwise may even refuse to eat the leaves.

You must also examine the undersides of the leaves carefully, especially during the late summer, because spiders sometimes lay their eggs on them. A part of the leaf is often folded over to disguise the presence of the brood, which could have catastrophic effects on a group of newly hatched nymphs. The introduction of older spiders on the food plant can also lead to losses of nymphs.

Occasionally, leaves are soiled with bird droppings. Such leaves should not be used for feeding purposes but should be trimmed off the branch. The leaves themselves will generally stay fresher if they are left attached on a stem. This will also provide the necessary height in the unit so that moulting can take place without undue difficulty.

It is certainly worth rinsing the leaves under the cold water tap for a few moments to remove any obvious dirt before offering the stem to the stick insects. The remaining water droplets also provide a source of drinking water. Some stick insects appear to have a higher water consumption than others. The *Eurycantha* species will even drink from a shallow open pot of water in their quarters.

You can experiment within reason to see if your stick insects will sample other greenstuff aside from bramble. The Javanese, for example, often shows a preference for rhododendron leaves, as does the Reunion Green Stick Insect (*Raphiderus scabrosus*), although both will take bramble.

Privet can be offered to various species, being a particular favorite of the Indian, which will also eat ivy. Both these plants are essentially evergreen, and so can be obtained without too much difficulty throughout the year.

Most species of stick insects prove not too selective regarding their diet, and it is best to feed a variety of foods to ensure sound nutrition.

More seasonal offerings are rose leaves and those of oak, which, incidentally, are the preferred food plants of leaf insects (*Phyllium* species). In addition, pyracantha is being used more widely as a winter food by many stick insect breeders, although it may be harder to provide adequate quantities of this shrub, compared with bramble.

The vast majority of stick insects, particularly those that have been commercially cultured, will thrive on any or all of the above plants. Only a few species have proved to be fussy about their diet, and, in time, they can often be weaned to more readily available substitutes, rather than guava leaves or tropical ferns, for example.

If you have access to the species' natural food, such as eucalyptus, then you may nevertheless find that your culture thrives better as a result. The offspring are likely to be bigger and may also tend to grow more rapidly. If you change their diet, try to do this after a moult, when the new food plant is more likely to be accepted.

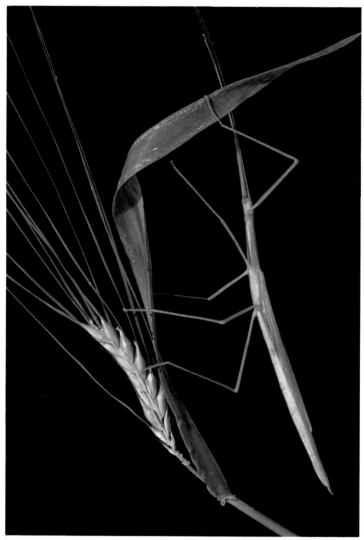

Pink-winged Stick Insect inspecting a potential meal. Photo by M. Gilroy.

FEEDING REGIMEN

Stick insects should have a supply of food constantly available to them, and, although you can gather it fresh every day, this is not strictly necessary. Apart from being time-consuming, it is also wasteful of precious food stocks which may run short later in the year as a result.

Instead, cut a reasonable length of bramble, for example, which will just be tall enough to fit inside the cage. Then make a vertical slit at the base of the cut stem. This serves to improve water uptake, and hence prolongs the freshness of the stem and its leaves, which are then unlikely to wilt for two or three days, depending on the temperature.

It is vital to choose a narrow-necked yet stable container for the stems. The larger stick insects, such as the female Jungle Nymph, are surprisingly heavy and may cause an unstable vessel to tip over, flooding the floor of the cage with water as a result. In contrast, if the neck is too wide, the stick insects, especially nymphs, may fall in through the gap and drown.

Having set the stem in water, it is worthwhile to fix either a cotton-wool or paper tissue plug around the neck of the vessel. This prevents the stick insects from having direct access to the water, although they can still take advantage of the moisture. As an alternative to placing the stems in water, some breeders prefer to use damp sand. But, in order to ensure the stability of the stems, the sand must be several inches deep, and there is really no benefit in this method.

You will soon come to appreciate the quantity of food that your stick insects are eating each day. Try therefore to provide sufficient food, but not excessive, which would simply be wasteful. Discard the stem once the leaves start to wilt, and before they can turn mouldy.

In addition to the food plant, you can also decorate the cage with dried twigs. Twigs serve to give the stick insects more scope for exercise, and, unlike the food plant, are unlikely to become mouldy. Of course, if you have your own food supply established and the surroundings are sufficiently large, then you can simply place the plant in its pot inside the cage. Keep it watered as usual, removing it to recover before the stick insects have stripped off all the leaves.

WATER AND HUMIDITY

For species that do actually drink, such as the *Eurycantha* stick insects, you will need to provide a very shallow dish of water. The clean plastic lid off a coffee jar can be used as a water vessel, although it is unwise to fill it to its maximum capacity. Stick insects are prone to drown in unguarded pots of water, especially at an early age.

Tropical species usually benefit from a higher humidity level than those originating in temperate or very arid areas. As a result, it can be beneficial to spray lightly the quarters of tropical insects on a regular basis. A plant sprayer is ideal for this purpose, but obviously you must be certain that it has not been used previously for dispensing any insecticide compounds, as these could harm your stick insects if any residues remain.

Tepid water is to be recommended for spraying, as cold water can have a chilling effect. If the stick insects are laying, it is probably better just to spray the food plant outside the cage. Should the base of the cage become damp, the eggs are likely to be affected by mould. There is no need to saturate the leaves in any event. This could prove fatal for recently hatched nymphs. Some breeders do not routinely spray the food plants, allowing the stick insects to obtain sufficient moisture from their food. But, if the stick insects are housed in a room with central heating, it is likely that they will require extra fluid provided by this means. You can keep a check on the humidity level within their quarters quite easily by means of a hygrometer gauge, available from many garden centers and similar outlets. This fits onto the front of the unit and can be read easily, indicating whether the atmospheric conditions are too dry.

CLEANING

You will need to change the floor covering about twice a week in most cases, depending on how many stick insects are in the cage. Paper can just be folded up and lifted from the edges so that the droppings are easily contained.

It is obviously a good time to clean out the cage when you replace the food plant; but, before discarding the plant, check that there are no small nymphs concealed on it. In addition, with the Pink-winged, you will need to examine the individual leaves carefully, as this particular species will lay its eggs among them, and you could discard them accidentally.

MOULTING

As stick insect nymphs grow, they shed their skins at regular intervals until they reach adulthood. The number of moults varies somewhat according to the species and the individual's gender. Male Giant Prickly Stick Insects, for example, undergo five moults, whereas females shed their skins six times, as do Indian Stick Insects. This could be linked to the fact that males generally mature earlier than females.

Moulting is also dependent on temperature to some extent, although it may be more an indication of food intake and a subsequently increased rate of growth. Not surprisingly, stick insects kept at a higher temperature tend to moult more than those of the same species kept at what could be considered a sub-optimal level.

Before moulting, stick insects tend to become less active and

This Giant Spiny stick insect has suffered a bad moult. Note the remaining skin on the insect's right rear leg.

may lose their appetite for a day or so. This is especially evident in larger species immediately prior to the adult moult. The insect typically hangs upside down off a convenient branch or stem, and, following a series of contractions, the skin in the vicinity of the top of the thorax splits in a straight line. The stick insect then slowly emerges head first through this gap, and at once the dramatic increase in its size is apparent.

It will then rest for a period, before finally climbing forth, pulling its abdomen out of its old skin. The stick insect then remains inert for several hours, until the new skin has begun to harden. Avoid handling recently moulted stick insects at this stage, for they can be easily injured. In some cases, the insect will consume its old skin, although generally it is ignored.

33

LIFESPAN

Having moulted for the last time, stick insects enter the last phase in their life cycle. For males, this period is usually brief, unlikely to exceed a month or so in many species. Males often die soon after mating. In contrast, some females may survive for well over six months as adults, laying eggs for much of this time.

Older stick insects approaching the end of their life tend to require more fluid. Prior to death, they become more inactive and then simply fall to the floor. It is possible to preserve them in a similar way to preserving butterflies, but their bodies prove exceptionally fragile, and wings and limbs are very easily broken. You can obtain entomological pins for mounting purposes from butterfly farms, and even special display cabinets.

DISEASES

Stick insects are not prone to illness in captivity, although, in the wild, as mentioned previously, the various stages in the life cycle are all susceptible to parasites. Both eggs and adults can be infected with fungal diseases, which usually arise in collections because of overcrowding, poor

Male Jungle Nymph, *Heteropteryx dilatata*.

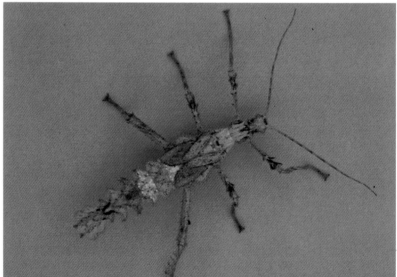

ventilation and unsanitary conditions. The remedy is obvious, with husbandry practices needing rapid improvement.

Injured stick insects, especially those lacking more than one limb, can also develop fungal infections. There is really no effective treatment, and badly injured insects should be euthanised painlessly. Freezing is the most commonly recommended procedure of euthanasia.

Some losses are likely during the moulting periods, especially with young nymphs. But widespread losses should be a particular cause for concern. Assuming that the humidity is adequate, then the food supply should be checked. It might be that this is polluted in some way, with insecticides, for example. As a precautionary measure, replace all food with a new supply from a fresh locality. Assuming that the losses then cease, this will be a good indication of the source of the problem.

Giant Prickly nymph using its scorpion-mimicking defence behavior. Besides predation, most nymph losses in the wild occur because of bad moulting.

Alternatively, it could be a factor in the local environment that is responsible. Although many stick insects come from warm parts of the world, you should never place them on a window sill in direct sunlight, especially if they are housed in a glass or acrylic tank, for the temperature inside will rapidly rise to a fatal level. Any stick insects that do manage to survive are likely to be badly dehydrated. Similarly, fly sprays used around the home can have especially insidious and lethal effects, and may even result in the death of all your stick insects. While you could remove them from the room before using a spray of this kind, remember that the deadly chemicals will be wafted around on air currents for some considerable time. They will remain a lingering hazard for your stick insects. As a result, it is therefore preferable to avoid using insecticide sprays in the same room as stick insects, and preferably in the rest of your home as well.

Stick insects can be injured easily by mishandling. Shown here is the proper way to pick up a mature stick insect.

HANDLING STICK INSECTS

Handling needs to be carried out gently at all times to avoid injury to the insect. Many stick insects can be encouraged to walk on your hand simply by placing a finger directly in front of them. They are then likely to climb onto your finger and progress quite rapidly up your arm. Their movement may cause a ticklish feeling, but it is not unpleasant.

You will have to take more care with some species than others. This applies especially in the case of the Giant Spiny, as well as female Jungle Nymphs, because of the sharp projections on their legs and body. Their defence can become noticeably apparent when you lift them up, as they will then press on your fingers.

Large nymphs and adult stick insects can be picked up without too much difficulty by restraining them gently on either side of their thorax, avoiding their legs. Nevertheless, the legs are likely to be anchored firmly around the plant, for example where the stick insect was resting. If you simply try to lift the stick insect off, you will almost certainly damage one or more of its legs. Instead, you will need to pry off the legs carefully, using a blunt object such as part of a cocktail stick to dislodge the grip of its claws. It may prove easier to encourage the stick insect to walk onto your open hand by placing it in front of the insect.

Take particular care with stick insects which have recently moulted, as their bodies will still be very soft. Never press on a stick insect's body with your finger in any event, because this could cause serious internal injury.

Young nymphs are especially difficult to handle, by virtue of their small size. Should you need to move them, it is often easiest to persuade them to walk onto a large leaf. Alternatively, you can transfer them by means of a small paint brush. Place the brush under the nymph. Once it has gripped onto the bristles, you can move it elsewhere, without fear of injuring it.

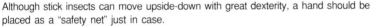

Although stick insects can move upside-down with great dexterity, a hand should be placed as a "safety net" just in case.

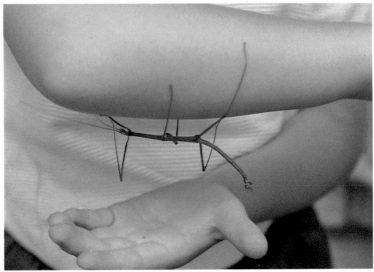

All stick insects reproduce by means of eggs, usually referred to as ova. In some species, such as the Indian, the population is comprised almost entirely of females. They in turn reproduce without mating–this is described technically as parthenogenesis. On the rare occasions when males are seen in this particular species, they do not appear to mate with females.

BREEDING

Some stick insects reproduce parthenogenetically in certain areas and sexually in other parts of their range. This applies in the case of the European Stick Insect (*Bacillus rossius*), which is widely distributed in the northern Mediterranean region.

Populations in the southern parts of France and northwestern Italy are parthenogenetic, with virtually no males present, while elsewhere–in southern Italy, for example–both sexes occur and mate together. There are also areas of overlap, where both parthenogenetic and sexual reproduction can take place. The hatchability of eggs produced by mating is generally higher than those produced parthenogenetically.

Provided that you have several female stick insects, there is a good possibility that they will breed quite successfully on their own, depending to some extent on the species concerned.

SEXING AND MATING

In many cases, there is a distinct difference in size between adult male and female stick insects. Females are often considerably bigger than their partners, both in terms of length and width. Often there are also clear differences in structure at the rear end of the abdomen. That of the male is relatively square, whereas the female's has a somewhat pointed tip, which is the ovipositor through which the eggs are laid.

When mating occurs, there is no preliminary courtship or any sign of aggression between rival mates. Attracted by the female's scent, a male simply climbs onto her back and loops his abdomen around to form a union with her. They may stay together like this for a number of hours and mate repeatedly over a period of time.

Facing page: Newly hatched stick insect. Photo by M. Gilroy.

In some species, such as the Giant Prickly, the transfer of the sperm in a packet known as a spermatophore is often visible. The whitish spermatophore may be evident close to the genital opening of the female after mating has taken place. Female stick insects are able to store sperm in their bodies, so a single mating can fertilize eggs laid over a period of months.

In species that are also capable of parthenogenesis, the female stick insect will continue to produce eggs even after all the sperm have been utilized. This can be detected because, instead of producing nymphs of both sexes, her parthenogenetic offspring are likely to be all female.

EGG LAYING

Female stick insects lay their eggs in various ways, depending on the species concerned. Many simply appear to scatter their eggs at random around their quarters. You are unlikely to see any eggs until several weeks after the insect has moulted for the last time. But then, throughout most of the remainder of their lives, females will continue laying regularly.

The number of eggs produced is usually quite large. Giant Prickly Stick Insects have proved amongst the most prolific, with mated females regularly producing as many as 1,000 eggs. Parthenogenetic individuals may lay slightly fewer. Various factors influence egg output. A good supply of food and spacious surroundings appear to exert a positive effect, increasing the numbers laid. Those species that tend to live longer also have a higher reproductive capacity; but, in all cases, females are likely to lay no fewer than 100 eggs.

Some female stick insects forcefully eject their eggs. The Giant Prickly is a typical example, which, by flexing the tip of its abdomen forward under its body, fires out eggs below its head. This method of egg dispersal probably helps to ensure that the nymphs are more widely distributed when they hatch, and so are less likely to be in competition with each other for food. The range can be quite surprising. Eggs may be ejected nearly 20ft (6m) in the case of *Cyphocrania gigas*, as one example.

Some stick insects actually conceal their eggs. The Javanese prefers to lay its eggs in crevices, where they are more likely to be out of reach of predators. Others, such as the Florida Stick, go to great lengths to bury their eggs. Females in this case excavate a shallow hole in which they lay up to ten eggs. Interestingly, the abdomen is curled over the head as egg laying takes place, with the eggs falling forward into the hollow. Finally, the insect covers up its nest by scraping soil over the eggs with its legs.

Giant Spiny Stick Insects also bury their eggs but tend to lay each one in a separate locality. While egg-scatters present no particular

Resembling seeds in appearance, these stick insect eggs are incubating on a bed of soil. Photo by M. Gilroy.

problems, you will need to provide a nesting area for species that lay their eggs below ground. Pots of sand or peat can be used for this purpose.

A clean empty yogurt container, with its sides cut down to about 2in (5cm) in height, should be placed in a reasonably accessible position in the cages of breeding females. You may see the female laying as she pushes her ovipositor into the container and then uses it to sweep over the surface to disguise the presence of the eggs beneath.

Breeders have also experimented with other media for egg-laying purposes. Some prefer to use the blocks of material used by florists for flower-arranging purposes. These tend to dry out less than the conventional media and also will not turn mouldy, which is likely to compromise the hatchability of the eggs. Others use gardening products made from volcanic rock, valued for their inert nature and water-retention properties. The particles in this case are relatively large, compared to sand, but can be offered in a container in a similar way.

Finally, some stick insects will actually glue their eggs around their quarters. The Pink-winged is the only species normally kept at present which displays this behaviour. It means that you will need to take particular care when changing over food plants, since it is not unusual to find eggs attached to the underside of leaves. Such eggs can be removed carefully with a small paint brush, but this is likely to have an adverse effect on their hatchability.

Instead, you can provide artificial sites for the females to lay their eggs. The drawback of allowing them to lay on the food plant is that this will turn mouldy while the eggs start to develop. They can sometimes be encouraged to distribute their eggs on a layer of bubble plastic (as sold in garden centers for insulation purposes). The layer can be pinned or taped up in their quarters quite easily and then transferred elsewhere for hatching purposes. Suspend the plastic down the sides of the cage, but avoid any light bulb, as the plastic will of course melt or even possibly catch fire if it is in close contact with a heat source.

The appearance of stick insect eggs is extremely variable. Many resemble seeds and can be confused with the seeds of the natural food plant of the species concerned. This obviously helps to disguise them in the wild from potential predators.

When you have females laying on the floor, it may be worth-while to clean the cage more often than usual. This will enable you to separate the eggs from the stick insects' droppings (sometimes known as 'frass') more easily. The eggs can then be transferred to new quarters to hatch. If you have several species housed together, then you may want to separate the eggs into different batches.

Apart from differing in appearance, eggs also vary quite widely in size. Those of the Indian Stick Insect are amongst the smallest, while the eggs of the Giant Prickly are considerably more sizable.

In spite of this diversity, however, you should be able to recognize all eggs easily by an obvious roof or lid, thru which the young nymph will ultimately emerge. This may be further emphasized by the presence of a knob, often described as the capitulum, on top of this operculum.

It can be helpful to provide supplementary heat for the eggs, as most appear to hatch better at a temperature between 70 and 84°F (21–29°C). Keeping them warm will also speed up the breeding cycle, although it can take anywhere from about two months to over one year for the young nymphs to emerge from their egg cases.

Male and female giant prickly Stick Insects in mating position. Photo by M. Gilroy.

Indian Stick Insect. This species appears to be parthenogenetic, meaning that mating need not take place as part of breeding. Photo by M. Gilroy.

The time taken also depends to some extent on the species concerned, and even eggs laid by the same female will not hatch simultaneously. In the wild, this could otherwise impose a strain on the food supply in the area, whereas more nymphs are likely to survive if they hatch over a period of time.

There is a further difference in the hatching process between stick insects from temperate areas and those normally found within the tropics. The ova of temperate species can remain over the winter without hatching, and so the period taken for the nymphs to emerge may be considerably longer.

By means of this arrested development, often labelled as a diapause, the nymphs will hatch the following spring. This population boost can prove significant if many of the older nymphs died as a result of a harsh winter. Eggs that have been fertilised tend to hatch much quicker in all cases.

In the case of the European species *Bacillus rossius*, the hatching period can vary from 60–280 days. Do not be tempted to discard eggs that appear slow to hatch, as they may well yield healthy, active nymphs at a later stage. Obviously, however, you will need to mark the batches of eggs so that you have an approximate idea of when they were laid, and can thereby estimate when they might hatch.

The percentage of ova that do hatch can be very variable. Obviously, this can be influenced by the conditions under which they were kept after laying, but this is not the only factor. Eggs from successive batches kept under identical conditions of temperature and humidity can produce quite diverse numbers of nymphs.

Fertilised eggs usually produce more offspring than those which are of parthenogenetic origin. In the case of species that normally mate prior to egg laying, this discrepancy can be very apparent. A study on the Javanese Stick Insect revealed that, while hatchability of fertilised eggs was about 81%, less than 5% of the parthenogenetic eggs yielded nymphs.

Some species have proved harder to breed successfully than others, and so not all that have been kept are now established in collections. Possible shortcomings in the adults' food supply and individual hatching requirements for the eggs are two factors that should be considered carefully if breeding results with one of the more unusual stick insects prove disappointing.

The eggs should certainly not be kept under conditions that are too dry, as this can be fatal to some species and slow the development of others, such as the Indian Stick Insect. But there is a risk that mould may develop on a culture that is kept over a period of time in conditions that are too moist, especially if the ventilation is poor. This can also devastate hatching.

As a precautionary measure, some breeders add a mould inhibitor to the substrate on which the eggs are resting. As a guide, sand tends to be less likely to support moulds than peat. A popular choice of chemical for inhibiting moulds is methyl-4-hydroxybenzoate. It may be possible to order this through a local pharmacy, rather than having to hunt out a manufacturer.

REARING THE NYMPHS

When the time for hatching comes, the nymphs emerge from the eggs: the operculum is pushed off, and the nymph squeezes out head first. It will appear rather like a miniaturised version of the adult, although young nymphs never have wings.

The first few days of life are a critical stage in the stick insect's development. The food plant must be easily accessible, close to where the nymphs are emerging. Avoid young juicy bramble leaves, however, because these seem to have an adverse reaction on some nymphs. Older, darker green leaves are to be preferred.

The tiny nymphs should not be handled if possible, because they are easily injured at this stage. They will tend to be more active after dark, when they would be less conspicuous to predators in the wild. The provision of adequate water is vital for those found in tropical areas, but take care if you are spraying their quarters. It is possible for tiny nymphs to drown in large water droplets.

In addition, species from North America and Europe generally prefer somewhat drier conditions than their tropical relatives. As a compromise, you can spray just one or two leaves lightly rather than the whole of the food plant.

If at all possible, try to provide a growing plant, rather than sprigs which will need to be replaced, as this will avoid the problem of transferring the nymphs from the old leaves to the new ones. If you do need to move them, however, then it is probably best to coax the nymphs onto a small piece of card or a fine paint brush. If you have a large number, however, this will prove a very time-consuming task.

With various nymphs of different species, you can house them together through the early stages at least, although it is a good idea to keep their quarters heated to about 75°F (24°C). This will encourage feeding activity and assist the growth and development of the nymphs.

Facing page: Philippine mantis eating his fellow insect, a cricket. Mantids will also eat stick insects, particularly nymphs, if given the chance. Photo by M. Gilroy.

Mature stick insect in the last stage of its lifecycle. Photo by M. Gilroy.

Some species, including the North American stick insects, can be housed satisfactorily in a warm room, if they are on their own.

As the nymphs grow larger, you will have to separate them into smaller groups, as they will need more space. If you see a number with damaged legs, then certainly they are overcrowded. Depending on your surroundings, you may find that you are in a position of having too many nymphs.

It will be best to seek new homes for them at an early stage. You can advertise them or approach a local pet shop to see if it would be interested in your surplus. Especially with the more unusual species, you should be able to place them without too much difficulty.

As they moult, it becomes easier to sex the nymphs. Young males are generally thinner than females of an equivalent age. In addition, the wings become increasingly apparent over successive moults, and this can provide a further means of distinction in some species, where males have bigger wings. Another useful indicator can be the presence of the egg-laying type of ovipositor in certain females, such as the Giant Spiny.

Jungle nymph showing its non-functional wings. This species is considered among the most spectacular of all Stick Insects currently available in the trade.

SPECIES

The following stick insects are being bred in commercial quantities, whereas there are many others that are presently kept by specialists who are trying to increase their numbers. The Phasmid Study Group has around 70 species that are being cultured by its members at present, and doubtless some of these will become more widely available in the future. The stick insects include the longest known insect in the world, namely P*harnacia serratipes*. The species is found in Indonesia, and females can grow to 13in (33cm) long. Doubtless this would make a fascinating subject for study should it become available. New species are regularly being added to the list of those which have already been kept.

Should you be fortunate enough to be involved in a project with such species, be sure to keep detailed records. By publishing your findings–in the newsletter of the Phasmid Study Group, for example–you will be helping to add to the knowledge about such species. Even observations on the more commonly kept stick insects can prove valuable to fellow enthusiasts.

INDIAN STICK INSECT (*CARAUSIUS MOROSUS*)

This species has been kept and studied since the beginning of the twentieth century. Its use in physiological experiments has earned it the alternative common name of Laboratory Stick Insect. This stick insect is very easy to keep, although it often proves more active after dark than during the daytime.

Adults tend to be quite variable in coloration, although they are often dull green. They measure about 4in (10cm) in length, and can be immediately distinguished by the red streaks at the top of their front legs. Although they are said to prefer privet, Indian Stick Insects can be fed and bred quite successfully on bramble alone.

The species is parthenogenetic, and although occasional males are found, mating does not appear to take place in any event. Males are

Facing Page: From South Vietnam comes the Annam Stick Insect. It is a rather delicate species that should be handled minimally.

While most other stick insects prefer high places, the Giant Spiny likes to conceal itself on the floor of its quarters.

smaller than females, with a red underside to their thorax. They also tend to be more active and have a shorter lifespan.

Females start laying their dark brownish eggs about a fortnight after moulting for the last time. These hatch readily at room temperature with no special attention after a period of four months or so. The nymphs moult into adults within five months and can live for one year.

PINK-WINGED STICK INSECT (*SIPYLOIDEA SIPYLUS*)

These active stick insects are widely distributed in Indonesia and New Guinea, as well as northern parts of Australia. The strain well-established in collections is based on stock from Madagascar, and, again, is comprised predominantly of females. The species is easy to accommodate, although there is a risk that their fragile wings could be torn on large bramble or rose thorns. These potential dangers should be removed before the food plant is placed in the insect's quarters.

Females are a similar size to those of the Indian Stick Insect, with males again being smaller. The eggs are stuck around their quarters and normally hatch rapidly, from six weeks onwards. Interestingly, the number produced is relatively small, probably because fewer are lost prior to hatching, as a result of the way that they are concealed.

The green nymphs are especially fragile, and they can prove reluctant to feed when they first hatch. Placing them in the company of older nymphs generally encourages them to start browsing. The other alternative is to introduce an adult to their quarters for this purpose.

After its final moult, the nymph will transform into the creamy-coloured adult. The pinkish wings are normally concealed along the back. Prior to flying, these stick insects often twitch their middle legs. They have an unusual defensive musky odor, which is likely to be apparent on your hands after handling them.

JAVANESE STICK INSECT (*ORXINES MACKLOTTII*)

The original stock of this attractive stick insect was obtained from the island of Java, located to the southeast of Malaysia. The Javanese has a somewhat delicate appearance but is relatively easy to maintain, although it prefers to feed on rhododendron rather than bramble. Adult females are slightly longer than males, growing to about 5in (13cm).

Coming from a tropical rainforest environment, this species

All species of stick insects make fascinating pets for children, but some are better suited to handling than others—and supervision is necessary.

The first stock of the distinctive Giant Spiny was obtained in New Guinea in 1978.

needs fairly humid and warm conditions. Spray the food plants daily, and keep these stick insects in a heated room. They are unable to fly using their wings, which serve as a defence against predators, with a flash of the orange markings concealed here proving an effective deterrent.

Provide a suitable container full of sand or a similar medium where the females can lay their eggs. Hatching takes at least five months, and, at first, the nymphs may be reluctant to feed. Keeping a group together, which includes older individuals, is the best means of overcoming this problem. They will often congregate in clusters.

Young females are quite difficult to recognize, but they tend to be broader than males. For breeding purposes, keep pairs in groups, although it appears that a tiny fraction of eggs laid by females housed on their own may hatch without mating.

GIANT PRICKLY STICK INSECT (*EXTATOSOMA TIARATUM*)

Also known as the Giant Spiny (not to be confused with *Eurycantha calarata*) and Mackay's Spectre, stock of this species is descended from that obtained during the 1960's, from Queensland, Australia. The species occurs through northern parts of Australia and is also present in New Guinea. Although it normally feeds on eucalyptus plants, bramble has proved an acceptable substitute.

Females can grow to at least 8in (20cm) long, with males averaging around 6in (15cm) in length. Whereas the wings of the female are never used, those of the male are both fully developed and functional.

In colour, eggs are a combination of gray and buff; they can take as long as nine months to hatch. They must be kept warm, at about 75°F (24°C) through this period, and also benefit from a reasonably humid environment. Hatchability in some cases may be poor.

Young nymphs are a dark reddish black shade, measuring about .5in (1.25cm) in length. They should also be housed at a temperature of around 75°F (24°C), although slightly cooler surroundings will not adversely affect them. Females can be distinguished at an early stage by their darker coloration and the presence of spikes on their abdomen. They will have moulted for the final time by five months of age and start mating soon afterwards. Parthenogenetic reproduction is not common in this species, and any eggs produced as a result will inevitably take much longer to hatch.

GIANT SPINY STICK INSECT (*EURYCANTHA CALARATA*)

These distinctive stick insects originate from New Guinea and neighboring offshore islands, including New Britain. The original stock was obtained during 1978, and, since then, it has become clear that the various populations differ somewhat in terms of their size. Females average about 6in (15cm) in length, while males measure around 5in (12cm) long and have a much longer spine on the upper part (the femur) of each of their hind legs.

Unlike most other stick insects, they usually prefer to conceal themselves on the floor of their quarters, under pieces of cork bark, newspaper and similar materials. Adults are dark brown in coloration, whereas nymphs are a variable shade of green. They will feed on a wide variety of plants, and even eat grass, although this, like other foods, must be free from chemicals.

Females will lay their eggs directly into pots. The eggs should be left undisturbed until they hatch, although it is preferable to move the pots to separate accommodations. The nymphs usually emerge about five or six months later. Separate them as they grow, especially as some males can prove aggressive towards each other when adults.

These stick insects should also be provided with a shallow dish of drinking water on a regular basis, because otherwise they are likely to become dehydrated. One of the longer-lived species, the Giant Spiny can have an adult lifespan of 1.5 years.

A very attractive female Jungle Nymph displaying its bright green coloration and rudimentary wings, which resemble small leaves.

Keepers of stick insects may be tempted to keep other insects as well. However, keeping stick insects with other species, even primarily herbivorous ones like this katydid, can create serious problems. Photo by M. Gilroy.

JUNGLE NYMPH (*HETEROPTERYX DILATATA*)

From the jungles of Malaysia comes one of the most spectacular species of stick insects currently available. Females in particular are an attractive and striking shade of bright green on their upperparts, and darker below. They have a rudimentary pair of wings, resembling small leaves, and a wide abdomen. Adult female Jungle Nymphs may measure nearly 7in (18cm) long. Males in comparison are much smaller and brownish in colour, with longer wings.

Bramble suits this species well as a basic diet, although it needs to be firmly held in place to support the weight of the females. Both sexes are essentially arboreal and do not spend much time on the ground. A temperature around 75°F (24°C) suits them well, with fair humidity, and a suitable safe supply of drinking water. They develop slowly, taking over one year before they are likely to start breeding. The eggs are buried and can take as long as 17 months to hatch. They need to be kept in warm and reasonably damp surroundings throughout this period. The nymphs can soon be sexed quite easily by the appearance of an ovipositor at the end of the abdomen in the case of females. It can prove one of the harder species to breed successfully, however, because a high percentage of the eggs often fail to hatch.

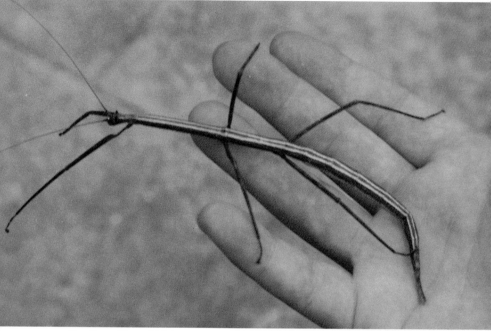

The Costa Rican Stick Insect is an interesting creature that has become well established in the fancy.

OTHER SPECIES

You may occasionally see various other stick insects offered for sale. One likely find is the Titan *(Acrophylla wuelfingi)*, another large Australian stick insect that originated from the state of Queensland. Both sexes have wings in this case but neither are active fliers. They are easily sexed, because females are significantly larger, measuring about 7in (18cm) long, and are pinkish brown, whereas males are predominantly dark brown. The Titan needs similar care to that suggested for the Giant Prickly. Eggs in this case can take a year to hatch, and some losses because of mould are likely to occur during this period.

Several species of stick insects have been bred from stock that originated from the Caribbean islands, including the fairly chunky Trinidad Log *(Creoxylus spinosus)*, which is brownish in color and grows to about 4in (10cm) or so. Males in this case have wings. Members of this species appear to like having branches in their quarters, as well as bramble and ivy, which are favored food plants.

Another even smaller stick insect from Trinidad is the Miniature (*Libethra regularis*). Males are very thin, whereas females are stockier. Both are brownish green in color. Again, bramble will be eaten by them quite readily. There is another species, originating from Jamaica, which is usually described just as the 'Unidentified West Indian Species', as it has yet to be classified. It is equally easy to keep and breed, however, with the brownish males being smaller in size than the green females, which also have a distinctive raised area on their abdomens.

Central and South American stick insects are also now becoming more commonly available. One that is well established is the Costa Rican (*Calynda brocki*). The female is chocolate brown in colour, with prominent white stripes on the upper surface of her body. Large females may measure nearly 6in (15cm). Males in contrast are considerably smaller, with prominent claspers on the tip of their abdomen which are used during mating.

Amongst Asiatic stick insects, a species from Thailand has yet to be properly classified, although stock has been bred by enthusiasts for over a decade. Females are usually greenish, whereas the dark brown males have distinctive white eyes. It has proved very prolific.

The Trinidad Log is a fairly broad stick insect native to the islands of the Caribbean.

Above: Eye of the Indian Stick Insect. Photo by M. Gilroy. **Facing Page:** The stick insects have earned a fancy that is dedicated to these fascinating creatures.

Another related species from this part of the world that you may encounter is the Annam, *Baculum* species. Females are brown, but considerably bigger than their partners, growing to about 4in (10cm) long. The males are rather easily injured, as with the Thai species, and should not be handled more than necessary.

Interestingly, there has been a tendency since this species was brought into collections from Annam in South Vietnam over two decades ago for stock to become increasingly parthenogenetic. So do not worry too much if you cannot obtain a male, as a percentage of the resulting eggs are likely to hatch in any event.

Finally, African stick insects have not proved as adaptable as those originating from elsewhere in the world. They are very rare at present, being only represented in specialist collections. Their dietary needs are generally far more specific. They tend to favour acacia, and a ready substitute has yet to be found for such plants.

Useful Address:

The Phasmid Study Group

c/o "Papillon" · 40 Thorndike Road · Slough · Berkshire SL2 1SR · England

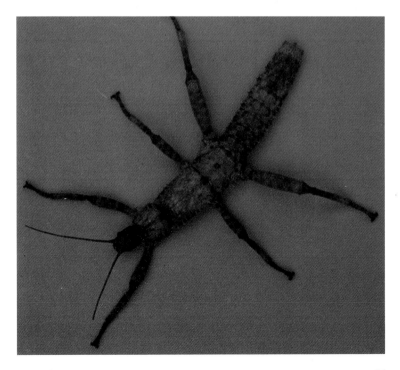

A fellow insect but certainly no proper companion to the stick insects: dead leaf mantis. Photo by M. Gilroy.

INDEX